DEMOS

GH00370615

www.demos.co.uk

Demos is an independent think tank committed to radical thinking on the long-term problems facing the UK and other advanced industrial societies.

It aims to develop ideas – both theoretical and practical – to help shape the politics of the twenty first century, and to improve the breadth and quality of political debate.

Demos publishes books and a regular journal and undertakes substantial empirical and policy oriented research projects. Demos is a registered charity.

In all its work Demos brings together people from a wide range of backgrounds in business, academia, government, the voluntary sector and the media to share and cross-fertilise ideas and experiences.

The Foreign Policy Centre

www.fpc.org.uk

The Foreign Policy Centre is an independent think-tank committed to developing innovative thinking and effective solutions for our increasingly interdependent world.

Foreign policy has never been more important in our lives. It governs everything from the jobs we do to the food we eat. We can no longer afford to see it as the work of diplomats alone. The Foreign Policy Centre will bring together all of the major actors in foreign policy – companies, charities, pressure groups and all government departments from the Home Office to the DTI. We will broaden perceptions of what foreign policy is, encourage public debate about our foreign policy goals and find new ways to get people involved.

The Foreign Policy Centre publishes books and reports, organises high-profile conferences, public lectures and seminars and runs major in-house research programmes on cross-cutting international issues.

THE POST-MODERN STATE AND THE WORLD ORDER

Robert Cooper

First published by Demos in 1996
Reprinted in 1998

Second edition published by Demos and
The Foreign Policy Centre in 2000

Demos
Panton House
25 Haymarket
London SW1Y 4EN
email: mail@demos.co.uk

The Foreign Policy Centre
Elizabeth House
39 York Road
London SE1 1NQ
email: info@fpc.org.uk

ISBN 1 84180 010 4 (2nd edition)
ISBN 1 898309 62 0 (1st edition)

Printed in Great Britain by Redwood Books, Trowbridge
Design by Lindsay Nash

CONTENTS

Foreword   vii

Introduction   1

The old world order   4

The new world order   10

The postmodern world   22

The postmodern state   31

The implications for security   34

Notes   44

Disclaimer

The opinions expressed in this book are the author's own and should not be taken as an expression of official government policy.

FOREWORD

Ten years after the end of the Cold War, we still have not found a name to describe the era we are living in, still less been able understand how it should work. George Bush's triumphant declaration of a new world order in 1990 soon gave way to a widespread sense of disorder, fuelled by ethnic warfare, resurgent nationalism and disintegration. The end of the nation state, global corporate rule and a clash of civilisations have all been predicted. Many commentators, stuck in a balance of power mindset, have spent eleven years speculating over which great power will fill the vacuum left by the USSR's collapse. The level of analytical confusion has reached the point where the American journal *Foreign Policy* has offered a cash prize to anyone who can invent a new term to encapsulate the age.

One problem with this search is that people are looking for a single description of a global system which is more diverse, variegated and complex than ever before. There are more wars, but they take place within states rather than between them. National governments struggle to deal with pollution, organised crime and refugee flows on their own, but work together in more effective and invasive international institutions. States have fragmented into smaller units and handed over many activities to the private sector, but are able to raise more money in taxes and offer better public services. More people have come out of poverty in the past 50 years than in the 500 before, but there has also been a massive increase in the gap between the richest and poorest.

Robert Cooper's pamphlet has had an enormous impact on this ongoing debate. It offers a nuanced, subtle and accurate analysis of the new world of foreign affairs. Its starting point is the claim that 1989 was a revolutionary year, the end both of a 50-year Cold War, and of a 300-year period defined by the balance of power between states. The analysis would have been unusually stimulating and radical whoever had written it, but the fact that it came (in a personal capacity) from a serving British diplomat makes it unique. Cooper has been described by *New Republic* as the foremost commentator on strategic issues of our age. His new role in the Defence and Overseas Secretariat of the British Cabinet Office ensures that his original insights continue to shape policy and strategy.

In this second edition, Cooper updates his argument and offers new material on the role of religion and democracy in international politics. He argues that we are witnessing the transformation – not the demise – of the nation state, and the emergence of an entirely new form of order, in which states defend their interests through mutual vulnerability, pooled sovereignty and transparency. However, this new form of order applies only to a handful of 'postmodern' states, operating alongside the modern - such as Brazil and China, still primarily concerned with their own sovereignty and maintaining regional balances of power - and the premodern, including Afghanistan and Sierra Leone, which are unable to achieve basic conditions of statehood, such as sustaining the rule of law.

Cooper's most important prediction in 1996 was that foreign policy challenges would flow not from the rise of a great power, but from the interaction between these different kinds of state. Events, from the humanitarian catastrophe in Kosovo to nuclear testing in the Asian subcontinent, drug production in Burma and Columbia to currency crises in Thailand and Brazil, have proved him right. Such events have brought pre-modern, modern and postmodern countries together in new and unpredictable ways. They have demonstrated further that the old rules and theories of international relations, devised for a balance of power system, are unable to guide us in this new era.

The most important question to arise from this analysis – what is the guiding purpose of foreign policy in the absence of Cold War certainties? – is yet to be answered convincingly. The absence of a clear answer helps to explain some of the British government's difficulties in articulating a sound basis for its 'ethical' foreign policy. The pamphlet provides a much-needed context for this ongoing debate. It also makes it clear that the eventual answer will depend partly on a new account of the domestic, or internal, functions of the state. This is because the balance-of-power system relied on a conception of the domestic state – with clearly defined borders, a monopoly on legitimate violence and strong, highly centralised systems of administration and service provision – which reached its apex during the middle decades of the twentieth century. The transition to a new definition of statehood, in which states invest more in the human and social capital of their citizens, and accept that they will be more mobile and less subject to coercion, is in its early stages. It is unlikely to lead to the disappearance of the state from domestic life, but it does imply that its tools of intervention and the sources of legitimacy will be very different.

Cooper's analysis also points powerfully to a series of challenges for the future. The first is global governance. The argument suggests that, in the long run, security and prosperity will be strengthened by achieving postmodern status for larger areas of the world. This conflicts with the current priority, which attempts to turn the United Nations into a form of global government. It is made more difficult by the complaint from modern states that current multilateral institutions, from the UN to the WTO, are rigged in favour of the old powers. To complicate the challenge still further, the sustained intervention by postmodern nations in pre-modern zones, such as Kosovo and sub-Saharan Africa, is both difficult to legitimate with sceptical publics and hard to justify in terms of effectiveness. One challenge is to open up multilateral institutions to give other countries a sense of ownership, without paralysing the institutions from acting when necessary. This surely depends on gearing intervention towards preventive action and the long-term development of democratic systems and cultures, rather than rapid reactions to immediate crises.

Second, non-state actors will play an important role in the new system, but what this role should be is not yet clear. Traditionally, states were the only actors that mattered in world politics. But what happens to the picture when half of the world's largest economies are companies rather than countries? How should states respond to globally organised protest movements, sometimes fuelled by NGOs which claim millions of members? Governments clearly have a new role to play in brokering and mediating these relationships, which will infuence future global governance structures and help to shape the debate over corporate social responsibility.

Third, the place of morality in international affairs. Cooper argues that we should abandon the centuries-old moral distinction between the internal and external uses of force. Cooper interprets Machiavelli's doctrine as arguing that, in external affairs, the moral precepts guiding domestic policy do not apply: lying, cheating and deception were both necessary and acceptable. But such a distinction can only be sustained when there is a clear boundary between home and abroad, as there was under the balance of powers system. Under the new conditions, it becomes untenable. Not only are domestic and international politics increasingly intermeshed, but postmodern states may find themselves trying to apply one set of principles to their peers, where security is based on mutual respect and interdependence, and another to dealings with modern states. The need for such double standards makes an 'ethical foreign policy' difficult to articulate and defend, as New Labour has discovered.

This is doubly important because of the clear need to construct the basis for a new, international, moral order. Such a foundation will have to move us beyond the defeatist rhetoric of the 'clash of civilisations' and the cop-out of moral relativism. In practice, much common ground has already been established. No mainstream culture or religion supports genocide or mass murder. Most countries have signed the Universal Declaration of Human Rights, support the idea of democracy and have joined multilateral institutions which protect basic rights.There are of course genuine differences which will be difficult to breach. But, as Cooper shows, it is impossible for states to ignore their interdependence, when everything from refugees and environmental pollution to genetically modified food flows across their borders. Achieving genuine moral dialogue, rather than preaching at their neighbours, is a key challenge for postmodern states.

The Postmodern State and the World Order does not provide answers to these challenges. But the framework that it offers illuminates the field of foreign affairs, and offers incision and clarity amidst crowded and confused debate. As we tackle the challenges of the twenty-first century, its reputation is likely to grow.

Tom Bentley **Mark Leonard**
Demos *The Foreign Policy Centre*

INTRODUCTION

Nineteen-eighty-nine marked a break in European history. What happened in 1989 was in some respects more far-reaching than the events of 1789, 1815 or 1919. These dates, like 1989, stand for revolutions, the break-up of empires and the re-ordering of spheres of influence. But until 1989, change took place within the established framework of the balance of power and the sovereign independent state. Nineteen-eighty-nine was different. In addition to the dramatic changes of that year – the revolutions and the re-ordering of alliances – it marked an underlying change in the European state system itself.

To put it crudely, what happened in 1989 was not just the end of the Cold War, but also the end of the balance-of-power system in Europe. This change is less obvious and less dramatic than the lifting of the Iron Curtain or the fall of the Berlin Wall, but it is no less important. And, in fact, the change in the system is closely associated with both of these events and perhaps was even a precondition for them.

Historically, the best point of comparison is 1648, the end of the Thirty Years' War when the modern European state system emerged at the Peace of Westphalia. 1989 marked a similar break point in Europe. What is now emerging into the daylight is not a re-arrangement of the old system but a new system. Behind this lies a new form of statehood, or at least states which are behaving in a radically different way from the past. Alliances which survive in peace as well as in war, interference in each other's domestic affairs and the acceptance of jurisdiction of international courts mean that states today are less absolute in their sovereignty and independence than before.

In a curious symmetry these changes have come about partly as a result of a second thirty years' war: 1914 to 1945. The First and Second World Wars brought a level of destruction which Europe had not seen since the first Thirty Years' War. The other factor was the nuclear confrontation of the Cold War: this offered the possibility of devastation on a scale without historical precedent. At the same time, it froze Europe for 40 years but thereby also allowed a breathing space for new ideas and new systems to emerge. A change in the state system in Europe was clearly required: if the existing system was producing such unacceptable levels of actual and potential destruction, it was not performing its function. We should not, therefore, be surprised to see a new system emerging.

Thinking about foreign affairs – like any other kind of thinking – requires a conceptual map which, as maps do, simplifies the landscape and focuses on the main features. Before 1648, the key concept was Christendom; afterwards, it was the balance-of-power. Since 1648, the European order, and the policies that predominated within it, have been given a variety of names: the concert of Europe, collective security, containment. Each of these was in fact the name for a variation on the balance-of-power (collective security was a special and particularly unsuccessful variation). If, as this essay argues, Europe has now moved beyond the balance-of-power system, we need to understand the new system on which our security is now based. It requires a new vocabulary and, up to a point, new policies.

A particular problem in understanding the international system – as opposed to the European system – is that it has become less unified since the end of the Cold War.

The Cold War brought the international system together in a global confrontation and seemed to invest even obscure corners of the world with strategic importance. Most foreign policy issues could be viewed in the light of a single overwhelming question. With the end of the Cold War this rather artificial unity of vision has been lost. Unity has also been lost in a second sense. As will be argued later on, while Europe is developing a new and more orderly security system, other parts of the world are becoming, if anything, more disorderly. It was perhaps natural that with one global order gone, statesmen should want to hail the arrival of a new world order. But, as is now obvious, this is a poor description of the actual state of affairs.

Understanding the kind of world we live in is important. The costs of intellectual errors in foreign affairs are enormous. Wars are sometimes fought by mistake. Suez was a mistake, at least for Britain: it was fought on the theory that Nasser was a new Hitler, to defeat a threat to order, but neither the threat nor the order really existed. Algeria was a mistake: it was fought for a concept of the state that was no longer sustainable. Vietnam was a mistake: the United States thought it was fighting the Cold War, when in practice it was continuing a French colonial campaign. These conceptual errors had heavy costs. Clarity of thought is a contribution to peace.

The purpose of this essay is to explain the changes that have taken place and to offer a framework for understanding the post-Cold War world. The central focus will be on Europe, for a number of reasons. It is Europe that has dominated, first actively and then passively, the international stage for about 500 years. Secondly, it is in Europe that systemic change has taken place: the nation state balance-of-power system came into being first in Europe; and now the post-balance system (which I call the postmodern) has also begun in Europe. Thirdly, this essay is written primarily for Europeans; they face the twin challenge of making the new model of security work on their own continent while living with a world that continues to operate on the old rules.

THE OLD WORLD ORDER

To understand the present we must first understand the past. In a sense, the past is still with us. International order used to be based either on hegemony or on balance. Hegemony came first. In the ancient world order meant empire: Alexander's Empire, the Roman Empire, the Mogul, Ottoman or Chinese Empires. The choice, for the ancient and medieval worlds, was between empire and chaos. In those days imperialism was not a dirty word. Those within the empire had order, culture and civilisation. Outside the empire were barbarians, chaos and disorder.

The image of peace and order through a single hegemonic power centre has remained strong ever since. It was long present in dreams of the restoration of Christendom or in proposals for world government; it is still visible today in calls for a United States of Europe. The idea of the United Nations as a world government (which it was never intended to be) still survives; at least the UN is often criticised for failing to be one.

However, it was not the empires but the small states that proved to be a dynamic force in the world. Empires are ill-designed for promoting change. Holding the empire together – and it is the essence of empires that they are diverse – usually requires an authoritarian political style; innovation, especially in society and politics, would lead to instability. Historically, empires have generally been static.

Europe's world leadership came out of that uniquely European contribution, the small state. In Europe, a third way was found between the stasis of chaos and the stasis of empire. In the particular circumstances of medieval Europe, empire had become loose and fragmented. A tangled mass of jurisdictions competed for control: land-owners, free cities, holders of feudal rights, guilds and the king. Above all the Church, representing what remained of the Christian empire, still held considerable power and authority competing with the secular powers.

The success of the small state came from its achievement in concentrating power – especially the power to make and to enforce the law – at a single point: that is to say in the establishment of sovereignty. Unlike the Church, whose claim was to universal rule, the state's secular authority was limited geographically. Thus Europe changed from a weak system of universal order to a pattern of stronger but geographically limited sovereign authorities without any overall framework of law. The war of all against all that Hobbes feared was prevented by the concentration of legitimate force at a series of single points; but both legitimacy and force were exclusive to single states. Domestic order was purchased at the price of international anarchy.

The diversity of the small European states created competition. And competition among the European states, sometimes in the form of war, was a source of progress: social, political and technological. The difficulty of the European state system, however, was that it was threatened on either side. On the one hand, there was the risk of war getting out of control and the system relapsing into chaos; on the other hand, there was a risk of a single power winning the wars and imposing a single hegemony on Europe.

The solution to this, the essential problem of a small state system, was the balance-of-power. This worked neither so perfectly nor so automatically as is sometimes imagined. The idea remains full of ambiguities. Nevertheless, whatever the inadequacies of the system, when it came to the point that the European state system was threatened by hegemonic ambitions from Spain, France or Germany, coalitions were put together to thwart those ambitions. This ran with the grain of the system: a sovereign power is naturally inclined to protect its sovereignty. This system also had a certain legitimacy: over the years, a consensus grew that the pluralism of European states should be maintained; and pluralism required balance. Some at least saw this as a condition of liberty in Europe.

With the balance of power went the doctrine of *raison d'etat*. Machiavelli had first put forward the proposition that the states should not be subject to the same moral constraints as individuals. This philosophy – that moral rules did not apply to states – was perhaps the counterpart of the changes by which the state ceased to be the private property of its ruler and at the same time reflected the breakdown of the Church's universal authority. Acceptance of *raison d'etat* grew from the Renaissance onwards until, by the end of the nineteenth century, it was the accepted wisdom and questions that had troubled Aquinas and Augustine about whether or not wars were just were no longer considered relevant.

Nevertheless, the balance-of-power had an inherent instability. It was the system in which a war was always waiting to happen. The end of the system came about as a result of three factors. The first was German unification in 1871. Here for the first time was a state that was too large and too dynamic to be contained within the traditional European system. Restraining German ambitions twice required the intervention of non-traditional European powers: the United States and the Soviet Union. And on the second occasion both remained behind in Europe, changing the nature of the system for ever.

The second factor was the change in technology in the late nineteenth century, which brought the industrial revolution on to the battlefield. War was inherent in the system; but by the beginning of the twentieth century, technology was raising the price of war to levels which could no longer be afforded.

The third change came with the second. The industrial revolution brought with it not just the means of moving the masses to the battlefield but also the mass society and democratic politics. This meant that war and peace could no longer be left to the judgements of a small and internationally-oriented elite. Balance-of-power thinking could be maintained in the Treaty of Utrecht or the Congress of Vienna or in Bismarck's Treaty with Austria after the War of 1866. But already in 1871 the influence of popular national feeling was playing a part; Bismarck's annexation of Alsace-Lorraine, against his own better judgement, showed that the Bismarckian days, when states could be juggled and balanced, had come to an end. By the time of the Versailles Conference, the kind of peace negotiations that Talleyrand and Metternich had conducted were no longer possible. The idea of the balance-of-power was already dead in 1919, although the Second World War saw one final coalition constructed to keep the European state system together.

If the European state system of the eighteenth and nineteenth centuries (and up to a point the first half of the twentieth century) was one of the balance-of-power, the world system was one of empires. The empires were, for the most part, the European system writ large. And the wars of empires – for example the Seven Years' War – were essentially European wars. Empires added prestige and provided background for European politics, whether in the Congress of Berlin or in the Agadir Incident; but the heart of the system still lay in Europe. That European powers had empires overseas was natural, but it was also a paradox. The paradox was that powers which operated a system of balance in their own continent – with its acceptance of national states and international pluralism – operated empires overseas suppressing nationalism and hostile to pluralism. This paradox was at the bottom of the unravelling of the empires in the second half of the twentieth century.

But empires were also natural. It is an assumption of the balance-of-power system that states are fundamentally aggressive, or at least that some states are aggressive some of the time. A system which is designed to thwart hegemonial ambitions makes the assumption that such ambitions are common. And, since balance in Europe prevented expansion there, it was natural for that expansion to take place overseas. This is another reason why Germany was a disturbing factor. By the time of Germany's emergence most of the available chaos had already been converted into empire (and some of the non-chaos, too) or had been declared empire-free (South America under the Monroe Doctrine). This left little room for Germany or Japan.

THE COLD WAR ORDER

The wars of 1914 to 1945 destroyed both the European balance-of-power in its traditional sense and also the European empires. The European empires depended on prestige, and this was fatally undermined in the Second World War. And in Europe itself, America and Russia were now needed to keep the system intact. What happened after 1945 was, however, not so much a radically new system as the concentration and culmination of the old one. The empires became spheres of influence of the superpowers. And the old multilateral balance-of-power in Europe became a bilateral balance of terror worldwide. In a strange way the old systems – balance in Europe and empire outside – were combined to produce something like a world order of balance between empires or blocs; a final culminating simplification of the balance-of-power.

The Cold War years were a period of wars and tension, but there was also an underlying order. This came in the shape of a tacit understanding that the USA and the USSR would not fight each other directly; nor would their major allies. Behind this, of course, lay nuclear weapons. The other side of this coin was that the Soviet Union was free to invade its own allies without Western interference. These unwritten rules also permitted the Soviets to arm North Vietnam, and America to arm Afghan guerillas; but neither sent conventional combat forces to a theatre where the other was committed. For the most part, the Cold War was fought with propaganda, bribery and subversion as much as in military combat. Where there was fighting, it was most often for political or ideological control of a particular country – Nicaragua, Angola or Korea, for example – rather than between countries. Many of the actual battles of the Cold War took place in civil wars. Thus the system had a certain orderliness since boundaries did not often change and major inter-state conflicts were usually outside the Cold War framework.

And yet the Cold War order was not built to last. Although it was stable on a military level it lacked legitimacy as a system. It was not just that many found the balance of terror repugnant – on the whole it was individuals rather than governments who had the moral doubts. Rather, the system lacked legitimacy. The ideologies of both sides rejected the division of the world into two camps; each claimed a universal validity and a moral authority for their system. (On the Western side this was probably more true in America than in Europe.) In this sense, the Cold War balance differed from the European balance-of-power system which was accepted by the governments of the day as legitimate and which, in some sense, matched the rationalist spirit of the times. The Cold War system never suited the more universalistic, moralistic spirit of the late twentieth century. Moreover both sides, within certain limits, were always ready to undermine it.

The end of the Cold War has brought not only the re-arrangement of the international scene that usually follows hegemonic wars but also domestic change. Since the Cold War was a battle of ideas as much as one between armies, those changes have not been imposed by occupying forces but introduced to willing, if bemused, governments by hordes of MIT-trained economists, management consultants, seminars and programmes of technical assistance (including the aptly named British Know How Fund). The unique character of the Cold War is also shown by the fact that instead of extracting reparations – a practice which lasted from the Middle Ages to the twentieth century – the victors have instead given aid to help convert the defeated side. Thus are wars of ideas different from wars of territory.

Ideas are not cost-free. They can be dangerous to peace. Democracy, the victorious idea in the Cold War, is a destroyer of empires. To run a democratic state with majority voting requires a strong sense of identity. Democracy entails the definition of a political community. In many cases, this has been provided by the idea of the nation. The break-up of the Soviet Union and of Yugoslavia, both in different ways Cold War empires, is a consequence of the victory of Western liberalism and democracy. The wars in those territories are democracy's wars. Liberalism and nationalism can go together today just as they did for eighteenth and nineteenth century states emerging from one or another form of imperial rule.

THE NEW WORLD ORDER

The point of this compressed historical survey is that we should understand that what came to an end in 1989 was not just the Cold War, nor
even in a formal sense the Second World War – since the 2+4 Treaty
(ending the post-war arrangements for Berlin and Germany) represents a
final settlement of that war, too. What came to an end in Europe (but
perhaps only in Europe) were the political systems of three centuries: the
balance-of-power and the imperial urge. The Cold War brought together
the system of balance and empire and made the world a single whole,
unified by a single struggle for supremacy and locked in a single balance
of terror. But both balance and empire have now ceased to be the ruling
concepts in Europe; and the world consequently no longer forms a single
political system.

THE PRE-MODERN

We live now in a divided world, but divided quite differently from the days
of the East–West confrontation. First there is a pre-modern world, the pre-
state, post-imperial chaos. Examples of this are Somalia, Afghanistan,
Liberia. The state no longer fulfils Weber's criterion of having the legitimate monopoly on the use of force. This circumstance may come about
because the state has in the past abused that monopoly and has lost its
legitimacy. In other cases, given the easy availability of conventional
weapons today, it may lose the monopoly. The state itself is a fragile structure, whether in primitive societies which may have less need of it, or in
complex urban and industrial societies which have a lower tolerance of
disorder but a more delicate structure of authority. The order provided by

the state is vital to society but if the state achieves order through domination it will stop society from functioning – as we have seen in Communist countries. As the fencing master says to his pupil in the film *Scaramouche,*[1] 'the rapier is like a bird. Grasp it too loosely and it will fly away, too tight and you will crush it.' So it is with the state and civil society.

The examples above are by no means the only cases of degeneration to a pre-modern state. It is early days since the end of the Cold War and more pre-modern states will emerge. Some areas of the former Soviet Union are candidates, including Chechnya, for all that it is part of Russia. All of the world's major drug-producing areas are part of the pre-modern world. In Afghanistan there is no real sovereign authority; nor is there in upcountry Burma or in some parts of South America, where drug barons threaten the state's monopoly on force. No area of the world is without its risky cases.

What is different today is that the imperial urge is dead in the countries most capable of imperialism. Land and natural resources (with the exception of oil), are no longer a source of power for the most technologically advanced countries. Governing people, especially potentially hostile people, is a burden. No one today wants to pay the costs of saving distant countries from ruin. The pre-modern world belongs, as it were, in a different time zone: here, as in the ancient world, the choice is again between empire or chaos. And today, because in the post Cold War world none of us sees the use of empires, we have chosen chaos.

As a result we have, for the first time since the nineteenth century, a *terra nullius.* It may remain so or it may not. The existence of such a zone of chaos is nothing new; but previously such areas, precisely because of their chaos, were isolated from the rest of the world. Not so today when a country without much law and order can still have an international airport.

While such countries no longer stimulate greed, they may excite pity: television pictures can bring their suffering into our homes. And, where the state is too weak to be dangerous, non-state actors may become too strong. If they become too dangerous for the established states to tolerate, it is possible to imagine a defensive imperialism. If non-state actors, notably drug, crime, or terrorist syndicates take to using non-state (that is, pre-modern) bases for attacks on the more orderly parts of the world, then the organised states may eventually have to respond. Occasionally they do so already.[2]

THE MODERN
The second part of the world is the modern. Here the classical state system remains intact. States retain the monopoly of force and may be prepared to use it against each other. If there is order in this part of the system it is because of a balance-of-power or because of the presence of hegemonic states which see an interest in maintaining the *status quo*. The modern world is for the most part orderly, but it remains full of risks. The Gulf, for example, is an area where it is necessary to think in balance-of-power terms. The Western concept has sometimes been of a balance between Iran and Iraq. Unfortunately, Iraq's emergence as the stronger power following the Iran–Iraq war brought that theory to an end, and (as in Europe in the first half of the century) the United States has been obliged to become the balancing element.

An important characteristic of the modern order (which I call 'modern' not because it is new – it is in fact very old-fashioned – but because it is linked to that great engine of modernisation, the nation state) is the recognition of state sovereignty and the consequent separation of domestic and foreign affairs, with a prohibition on external interference in the former. This is still a world in which the ultimate guarantor of security is force, a world in which, in theory at least, borders can be changed by force. It is not that, in the modern order, might is right so much as that right is not particularly relevant; might and *raison d'état* are the things that matter. In international relations, this is the world of the calculus of interests and forces described by Machiavelli and Clausewitz.

The concepts, values and vocabulary of the modern world still dominate our thinking in international relations. Palmerston's classic statement that Britain had no permanent friends or enemies but that only its interests were eternal is still quoted as though it were a lasting truth of universal application. Theories of international relations are still broadly based on these assumptions. This is clearly true for 'realist' theories, of the calculus of interests and the balance-of-power; it is also true for 'idealist' theories – based on the hope that the anarchy of nations can be replaced by the hegemony of a world government or a collective-security system.

The United Nations, as originally conceived, belongs to this universe. It is an attempt to establish law and order within the modern state system. The UN Charter emphasises state sovereignty on the one hand and aims to maintain order by force. The veto power is a device to ensure that the UN system does not take on more than it can handle by attacking the interests of the great powers. The UN was thus conceived to stabilise the order of states and not to create a fundamentally new order. This is not the whole story, since the charter also emphasises human rights and the United Nations has developed since its inception; but in conception the collective-security element of the UN Charter represents an attempt to throw the weight of the international system behind the *status quo*, so that the international community as a whole would become the balancing actor in the balance-of-power system.

Before passing on to the third element in the world system, it is worth noting that the modern order contains some worrying problems. The most notable feature is the lack of a real balance-of-power in many areas of the world. In the Gulf, we have already seen the consequences of that. But elsewhere there are also powerful states which might under certain circumstances become destabilising actors. India is one example, China another, Brazil a third.

None of these is directly threatening at the moment; for the most part they are preoccupied with economic development and with their own internal security and cohesion. That is also one reason why they hate external interference, which is both a challenge to state sovereignty and a threat to internal order. Any of these states could, if things went badly wrong for them, revert to a pre-modern state.

But it could be equally alarming if things went right for them. The establishment of internal cohesion has often been the prelude to external expansion. So it was for Britain after England and Scotland unified (the empire was always British), for Germany after 1871, for Japan after 1868. Both China and India, though they are part of the nation state system, have some of the characteristics of empires. Were they to develop the nation state's ability to concentrate loyalty and power they would be very formidable indeed. In fact, the arrival of any cohesive and powerful state

RELIGION AND THE RISE OF THE MODERN

Religion is intertwined in many ways in this story. Most empires are characterised by a strong religious element. Perhaps this is because the societies they have governed have been largely agrarian with the characteristic agrarian social structure of peasants, soldiers and priests. The eastern empire of Byzantium and the Western Carolingian empire were based on Christianity. The Ottoman and Mogul empires were based on Islam.

In the Russian empire Moscow was conceived as the third Rome; its subjects were identified by religion rather than ethnicity – Orthodoxy being the mainstream. Its successor, the Soviet empire, was founded on the secular religion of scientific socialism. Indonesia under Suharto – something between an empire and a nation state – employed the state ideology of Pancasila as well as the army to hold it together. Only China among the great empires seems to have been without an obvious religious element; the Chinese emperor was nevertheless the Son of Heaven and if things went wrong could lose its mandate.

Colonial empires are somewhat different. The European empires took with them a strong Christian element – missionaries often played a part in their creation – but Christianity was rarely used to establish the legitimacy of the Empire. Colonial empires are in any case a different kind of structure since the Imperial possessions are the possessions of a state rather than a part of it. The two do not together form a single unit of government: that is to say Britain was never a part of the British Empire.

The nation state, in contrast to an empire, is characteristically secular. Imperial rule is legitimised by the sanction of heaven; the emperor is appointed by God. National government is legitimised in the end by the nation: from below rather than from above. For a while, in Europe, kings borrowed the authority of the church and claimed that they held their appointments from above; but this was difficult to sustain over a long time: religions are universal and it is hard to explain why God should appoint so many different monarchs for independent sovereign states.

This logic took time to work its way through in Europe; but by the end of the twentieth century government is in practice almost entirely secular. A striking illustration is provided by Turkey where Ataturk, perhaps instinctively understanding the logic outlined above insisted that the Turkish state which he created out of the dissolving Ottoman empire should be secular. With the secularised state goes the amoral state of which Machiavelli was the prophet.

Although the legitimacy of emperors has a religious base empires are characterised by diversity including diversity of religions. Many of the subjects of the Mogul emperors were Hindus; the Russian emperor had Moslems as subjects and the Ottoman emperor Christians. In the colonial empires (which governed by technical and cultural superiority together with force rather than legitimacy) religion was also varied.

Empires usually come to an end as a result of military defeat. In the case of colonial empires, the end may also come as a result of changing circumstances in the colonising country (the case of post-War Britain or of Portugal for example). When an empire is defeated the most frequent result is break up. Occasionally one empire may be replaced by another as the Russian empire was replaced by the Soviet empire – something slightly similar happened in Indonesia following the Dutch withdrawal. But break up is more usual. When an empire breaks up the question of identity becomes relevant for the first time. Under an imperial power there is no requirement for its subjects to identify with it; in contrast a state, which is legitimised from below, requires some degree of identification from its citizens. National identities are usually created by states out of the raw material of history, culture, and language. Sometimes national identities may exist within an empire, where a historic memory survives (as it did in the Baltic States under Soviet rule). In certain cases it may have been fostered by the colonial power – as it was, up to a point, by Britain. Frequently this has proved weak in comparison with more deep-rooted (such as tribal) identities.

Where there is no other identification religion however provides a ready-made source of identity: it is fundamental in people's lives and their sense of who they are. It provides a strong sense of community. It is natural therefore that in a power vacuum left by retreating empire group loyalties should coalesce around religious beliefs. Hence, the regular occurrence of religious clashes where a retreating or weakening empire leaves a power vacuum.

The story in Europe is somewhat different. The Christian empire of western Europe, uniquely, divided itself into a spiritual component and a temporal component. The temporal empire ceased to be meaningful in the early Middle Ages but the spiritual component survived and while it did so it prevented the emergence of independent sovereign nation states. In theory at least the Pope had the power and the duty to adjudicate in disputes between states and was their hierarchical superior. The Treaties of Tordesilla and Saragossa which divided the world between Spain and Portugal were a late exercise of this role. (Even today the Papal Nuncio is still given precedence over the diplomatic representatives of other countries in certain European countries). The wars of religion in Europe were thus the cause rather than the consequence of the break up of the empire. It was the split in the Christian church and the wars that followed that finally lost Christendom its legitimising function. Thereafter, both power and legitimacy belonged to the states, and later to the nation atates, of Europe.

in many parts of the world could prove too much for any regional balance-of-power system to contain it.

There are many countries which could become too powerful or too aggressive for regional balance. The names mentioned are merely those of the largest regional actors; but we should not become too fixated by size. Internal cohesion and modern (especially nuclear) technology can compensate for small size, as, historically, the case of Britain demonstrates. In the pre-modern world, states (or rather would-be states) may be dangerous because they are failures; in the modern world, it is the successful states which are potentially dangerous.

It is even possible that we could see a new imperialism. Someone may decide to make some part of the chaos a non-white man's burden. If they do so, it will probably not be for economic reasons: taming chaos is not very profitable today – perhaps it never has been. Imperialism is more likely from defensive motives – when a nearby state of chaos becomes in some way a threat. Or imperialism may be in pursuit of an idea. To persuade your own people to risk their lives in chaotic foreign countries requires the belief that you are spreading some gospel, pursuing a mission of civilisation or (in the worst case) establishing the natural superiority of your race. It requires confidence and conviction. And then, if you are to be successful, you have to persuade the people that you are subjugating that you are doing this in their own interests and in the service of a higher good: most people are subjugated by ideas rather than by force. In this context, Islam is at least a possibility. A successful Islamist state is more likely to be a threat (or a saviour) for the pre-modern world than for Europe or the United States.

The conditions for the success of such a new imperialism are much more difficult today than in previous centuries. The new imperialists would encounter a national consciousness awakened, or created, by the previous generations of imperialists. They would also have to explain why the idea they offered was superior to the liberal/ capitalist/ consumerist democracy of the West. These are difficult challenges for a country aiming to establish a new empire; they might well make it impossible to sustain one.

A new imperialism from any of the modern states would not necessarily be damaging for Western interests, since it would be established in a zone that the West had chosen to abandon. More problematic would be the attempt to establish a regional hegemony. This might in the short run be threatening to Western interests and in the long run be threatening to the West itself. We have already seen such a threat in the Gulf; it is possible to imagine threats arising in the Pacific. If they did, in some years' time, will the West be equipped materially, psychologically and politically to deal with them? That brings us to the problem of postmodernity.

THE POSTMODERN

The third part of the international system may be called the postmodern element.[3] Here the state system of the modern world is also collapsing; but unlike the pre-modern it is collapsing into greater order rather than into disorder. Modern Europe was born with the Peace of Westphalia. postmodern Europe begins with two treaties. The first of these, the Treaty of Rome, was created out of the failures of the modern system: the balance-of-power which ceased to work and the nation state which took nationalism to destructive extremes. The Treaty of Rome is a conscious and successful attempt to go beyond the nation state.

The second foundation of the postmodern era is the Treaty on Conventional Forces in Europe (the CFE Treaty): this was born of the failures, wastes and absurdities of the Cold War. In aspiration at least the Organisation for Security and Cooperation in Europe (OSCE) also belongs to this world. So, in different ways, do the Chemical Weapons Convention (CWC), the Ottawa Convention banning anti-personnel mines and the treaty establishing an International Criminal Court.

The postmodern system does not rely on balance; nor does it emphasise sovereignty or the separation of domestic and foreign affairs. The European Union, for example, is a highly developed system for mutual interference in each other's domestic affairs, right down to beer and sausages. The CFE Treaty also breaks new ground in intrusion in areas normally within state sovereignty. Parties to the treaty have to notify the location of their heavy weapons (which are in any case limited by the treaty) and allow challenge inspections. Under this treaty, more than 50,000 items of heavy military equipment – tanks, artillery, helicopters and so on – have been destroyed by mutual agreement, surely an unprecedented event. The legitimate monopoly on force, which is the essence of statehood, is thus subject to international – but self-imposed – constraints.

It is important to realise what an extraordinary revolution this is. The normal logical behaviour of armed forces is to conceal their strength and hide their forces and equipment from potential enemies. Treaties to regulate such matters are an absurdity in strategic logic. In the first place, you do not reach agreements with enemies, since, if they are enemies they cannot be trusted. In the second place, you do not let the enemy come snooping round your bases counting weapons. What is it that has brought about this weird behaviour? The answer must be that behind the paradox of the CFE Treaty lies the equal and opposite paradox of the nuclear age: that in order to defend yourself you had to be prepared to destroy yourself. The shared interest of European countries in avoiding a nuclear catastrophe has proved enough to overcome the normal strategic logic of distrust and concealment. The mutual vulnerability that provided stability in the nuclear age has now been extended to the conventional end of the spectrum where it becomes mutual transparency. (The Cold War nuclear stalemate already contained some elements of the postmodern. It relied on transparency; for deterrence to work it has to be visible.)

The path towards this treaty was laid through one of the few real innovations in diplomacy – confidence-building measures. Through the fog of mistrust and deception, the Cold War states began to understand late in the day that the others might not, in fact, be planning to attack them. Measures to prevent war through miscalculation grew out of this, for example, observation of manoeuvres. The progression has proceeded logically to observation of weapons systems and to limitations on them. The solution to the prisoners' dilemma lies in ending mutual secrecy.

In one respect, the CFE Treaty collapsed at an early stage under its own contradictions. As originally designed, the treaty embodied the idea of balance between two opposing blocs. The underlying assumption was one of enmity: balance was required to make it unlikely that either side would take the risk of making an attack. Transparency was required to make sure that there was really a balance. But by the time you have achieved balance and transparency it is difficult to retain enmity. The result is that transparency remains but enmity and balance (and one of the blocs) have effectively gone. This was not, of course, the work of the

CFE Treaty alone but of the political revolution that made that treaty possible. It does suggest, however, that there is a basic incompatibility between the two systems; the modern based on balance and the post-modern based on openness do not co-exist well together.

Intrusive verification – which is at the heart of the CFE system – is a key element in a postmodern order where state sovereignty is no longer seen as an absolute. But far-reaching as they may be, the CFE Treaty and the CWC are only partial approaches towards a postmodern order.

Although their acceptance of intrusive verification breaks with the absolutist tradition of state sovereignty, the field in which sovereignty has been sacrificed is limited to foreign affairs and security. Thus what is permitted is interference in the domestic aspect of foreign affairs.

The aspirations of the OSCE go rather further. OSCE principles cover standards of domestic behaviour – democratic procedures, treatment of minorities, freedom of the press – which are distant from the traditional concerns of foreign and security policy. Whether the OSCE will develop – as it aspires to – into a system for international monitoring of domestic behaviour remains to be seen. If it does, this will be a break with the tradition of the European state system which will take all the OSCE countries (or all those who play by the rules) decisively into a postmodern world.

The characteristics of this world are:

- the breaking down of the distinction between domestic and foreign affairs
- mutual interference in (traditional) domestic affairs and mutual surveillance
- the rejection of force for resolving disputes and the consequent codification of rules of behaviour. These rules are self-enforced. No one compels states to obey CFE limits. They keep to them because of their individual interest in maintaining the collective system. In the same way the judgements of the European Court of Justice are implemented voluntarily, even when they are disliked, because all EC states have an interest in maintaining the rule of law
- the growing irrelevance of borders: this has come about both through the changing role of the state but also through missiles, motor cars

and satellites. Changes of borders are both less necessary and less important

- security is based on transparency, mutual openness, interdependence and mutual vulnerability.

The most prominent postmodern institutions are mentioned above but this list is by no means exclusive. The Strasbourg Court of Human Rights belongs in this category: it interferes directly in domestic jurisdiction. No less striking, within the Council of Europe framework is the Convention on Torture, which permits challenge inspection of prisons without warning and without visas. In the economic sphere, the IMF and the OECD operate systems of economic surveillance. The Non-Proliferation Treaty (NPT), taken together with the International Atomic Energy Agency (IAEA) safeguards and special inspection regimes, aspires to be a part of the postmodern system, although the lack of openness on the part of the nuclear powers themselves means that it does not fully qualify.

The International Criminal Court is a striking example of the postmodern breakdown of the distinction between domestic and foreign affairs. If the world is going to be governed by law rather than force then those who break the law will be treated as criminals. Thus, in the postmodern world, *raison d'etat* and the amorality of Machiavelli have been replaced by a moral consciousness that applies to international relations as well as to domestic affairs: hence also the renewed interest in the question of whether or not wars should be considered just.

The new security system of the postmodern world deals with the problems identified earlier that made the balance of power unworkable. By aiming to avoid war it takes account of the horrors of war that modern technology represents; indeed, it depends to a degree on the technology and on the horrors. It is also more compatible with democratic societies: the open society domestically is reflected in a more open international order. And finally, since security no longer depends on balance, it is able to incorporate large and potentially powerful states. The peaceful reunification of Germany is in itself a proof that the system has changed.

A difficulty for the postmodern state – though one that goes beyond the scope of this paper – is that democracy and democratic institutions are firmly wedded to the territorial state. The package of national identity, national territory, a national army, a national economy and national democratic institutions has been immensely successful. Economy, law-making and defence may be increasingly embedded in international frameworks, and the borders of territory may be less important, but identity and democratic institutions remain primarily national. These are the reasons why traditional states will remain the fundamental unit of international relations for the foreseeable future, even though they may have ceased to behave in traditional ways.

THE POSTMODERN WORLD

What is the origin of this change? The fundamental point is that 'the world's grown honest'.[4] A large number of the most powerful states no longer want to fight or to conquer. This gives rise both to the pre-modern and to the postmodern world. France no longer thinks of invading Germany or Italy although it has nuclear weapons, and these should theoretically put it in a position of overwhelming superiority. Nor does it think of invading Algeria to restore order there. Imperialism is dead, at least among the Western powers. Acquiring territory is no longer of interest. Acquiring subject populations would for most states be a nightmare.

This is not altogether a novelty. Imperialism has been dying slowly for a long time. Britain was inventing dominion status in the nineteenth century and – admittedly under intense pressure – was letting Ireland go early in the twentieth. Sweden acquiesced in Norwegian independence in 1905. What is, however, completely new is that Europe should consist of states which are no longer governed by the territorial imperative.

If this view is correct, it follows that we should not think of the European Union or even NATO as the reason we have had half a century of peace in Western Europe; at least not in the crude way that this is sometimes argued – that states which merge their industries or armies cannot fight each other. This proposition seems to be neither a necessary nor a sufficient condition for peace. After all the EFTA countries did not fight each other even though most were members of neither NATO nor the EU. And on the other side, Yugoslavia has shown that a single market and a single currency and integrated armed forces can be broken up if those concerned want to fight.

NATO and the EU have, nevertheless, played an important role in reinforcing and sustaining the basic fact that Western Europe countries no longer want to fight each other. NATO has promoted a greater degree of military openness than has ever existed before. Force planning is done in the open even if it is not quite so much a joint procedure as it is supposed to be. Joint exercises and an integrated command structure reinforce this openness. Thus within Western Europe, there has been a kind of internal CFE Treaty for many years – except that most of the times, states were urging each other to increase rather than to cut defence spending.

No doubt the solidarity created by having a common enemy also played a part initially; so did the presence of US forces, which enabled Germany to keep forces at lower levels than its strategic position would have warranted; and so did the US nuclear guarantee – which enabled Germany to remain non-nuclear. But for Germany to have pursued these policies in isolation would not have been enough: France or the UK might still have suspected a secret German troop build-up or a nuclear weapons programme. What mattered above all was the openness NATO created. NATO was and is, in short, a massive intra-western confidence-building measure.

This is why the reunification of Germany within NATO was so important. In a curious way, it is part of how NATO won the Cold War: not by beating Russia but by changing the strategic position of Germany. NATO provided a framework within which Germany – the epicentre of the Cold War – could be reunited. The balance-of-power system broke down in Europe because of Germany and, for a while, it seemed that the solution to the problem was to divide Germany. And – in the same logic – the Cold War was needed to maintain the division. Balance in Europe seemed to require a divided Germany and a divided Germany required a divided Europe. For Germany to be reunited, a different security system was required: in effect a post-balance, postmodern system, of which NATO was one key element.

The EU was another. Its security role is similar to that of NATO though this is harder to see since it is further from the sharp end of military hardware. It is not the Coal and Steel Authority (which did not integrate the industry so much as the market – German coal mines remained German and French steel mills remained French) that has kept the countries of

Europe from fighting each other, but the fact that they did not want to do so. Nevertheless, the existence of the Coal and Steel Authority and the Common Market and the Common Foreign and Security Policy and the Common Agricultural Policy and so forth, has served important reinforcing functions. They have introduced a new degree of openness hitherto unknown in Europe. And they have given rise to thousands of meetings of ministers and officials, so that all those concerned with decisions over peace and war know each other well.

They may or may not agree; they may or may not like each other, but they do belong to the same organisation and work together and make deals together over a wonderful range of subjects. By the standards of the past this represents an enormous degree of what might be called administrative integration. (This is neither complete political integration – which would require *inter alia* European political parties – nor economic integration, which takes place at the level of the firm, the investor and the workforce.) Again, compared with the past, it represents a quality of political relations and a stability in political relationships never known before. To create an international society, international socialisation is required and one of the important functions of the Brussels institutions is to provide this.

A second important function is to provide a framework for settling disputes between member states. Since force is no longer available some mixture of law, bargaining and arbitration is required: the EU provides this in most cases (not all since, for example, territorial disputes remain outside its ambit). The same framework of bargaining and law also regulates a good deal of transnational cooperation. As one (disappointed) observer noted, the EU is an organisation not for pursuing a European interest, but for pursuing national interests more effectively. In the postmodern context 'more effectively' means without being obliged to resort to military means.

The EU is the most developed example of a postmodern system. It represents security through transparency, and transparency through interdependence. The EU is more a transnational than a supra-national system. Although there are still some who dream of a European state (which would be supra-national), they are a minority today – if one takes account of ordinary people, a very small minority. The dream is one left over from a previous age. It rests on the assumption that nation states are fundamentally dangerous and that the only way to tame the anarchy of nations is to impose hegemony on them. It is curious that, having created a structure that is ideally adapted to the postmodern state, there are still enthusiasts who want to replace it with something more old-fashioned. If the nation state is a problem then the super-state is certainly not a solution.

Nevertheless it is unlikely that the EU, as it is at the start of the twenty-first century, has reached its final resting place. Perhaps the most important question is whether integration can remain a largely apolitical process. It is striking that monetary integration has been achieved precisely by removing monetary policy from the hands of politicians and handing it over to the technocrats. This may be no bad thing but, in the deeply democratic culture of Europe, the development of the EU as a continuation of diplomacy by other means rather than the continuation of politics by other means may in the end exact a price. International institutions need the loyalty of citizens just as state institutions do.

STATE INTERESTS

To say that the EU (or for that matter the Council of Europe or the OSCE) is a forum in which states pursue their interests should not be misunderstood. 'Interests' means something different for the modern state and for its postmodern successor. The 'interests' that Palmerston referred to as eternal were essentially security interests. They included such notions as the Russians should be kept out of the Mediterranean; no single power should be allowed to dominate the continent of Europe; the British Navy should be bigger than the next two largest navies combined and so forth. Even defined in these terms, interests are by no means eternal, though they can have a shelf-life measured in decades at least. These interests are defined by the security problems in a world of fundamentally predatory states. It is the essential business of a state to protect its citizens from invasion: hence the absolute, if not eternal, nature of these interests; hence the adjective 'vital'. Such interests still exist for the West today: it is probably a vital Western interest that no single country should come to dominate world oil supplies, perhaps also that nuclear weapons should not get into the hands of unstable, aggressive or irresponsible hands. Or if

Japan, for example, should come under serious military threat there would be a general Western interest, probably a vital interest, in defending it.

These are problems about encounters between the postmodern and modern world. Within the postmodern world, there are no security threats in the traditional sense; that is to say its members do not consider invading each other. The 'interests' that are debated with the European Union are essentially matters of policy preference and burden sharing. There is no fundamental reason why in the last GATT negotiations France should have been ready to sacrifice the interests of its software companies in favour of its farmers; France's 'interests' are defined by the political process. Such interests may change with governments. These are vested interests rather than national interests. In the UK, the Thatcher government brought with it a stronger commitment to open markets than its predecessor had shown. The 'interest' in free markets was born in 1979 – it was certainly not eternal. The vital national interests that are defended under the Luxembourg compromise are almost certainly neither vital nor national and they are not even 'interests' in the Palmerstonian sense – none of which is to say that they are unimportant.

If the second half of Palmerston's proposition, that interests are eternal, no longer applies in the postmodern world, the first half, that no country has permanent friends is equally alien. Although friendship is hardly a concept that applies between states, institutions like the EU and NATO constitute something analogous to a bond of marriage. In a world where nothing is absolute, permanent or irreversible, these relationships are at least more lasting than any state's interests. Perhaps they will even turn out to be genuinely permanent.

At all events we should beware of transferring the vocabulary of the modern world into the postmodern. Germany may (occasionally) exercise a dominant influence in the EU, or the USA may dominate NATO policy making, but this kind of dominance, achieved by persuasion or bought in some other way, is quite different from domination by military invasion. (These two countries are not, of course, mentioned by accident – but the significant fact in each case is probably not their size but the fact that they are dominant financial contributors to these two institutions.)

WHO BELONGS TO THE POSTMODERN WORLD?
It is certain that there is a new European order based on openness and mutual interference. The EU countries are clearly members. Whatever happens to the European Union, the state in Western Europe will never be the same again.

Although these postmodern characteristics apply among the states of the EU they do not necessarily apply between them and other states: if Argentina chooses to operate according to the rules of Clausewitz rather than those of Kant, Britain may have to respond on the same level. Similarly, in the days of the Cold War, all the European states had to operate on the old logic *vis-à-vis* the Warsaw Pact although among themselves the postmodern logic increasingly applied.

Outside Europe, who might be described as postmodern? Canada certainly; the USA up to a point perhaps. The USA is the more doubtful case since it is not clear that the US government or Congress accepts either the necessity and desirability of interdependence, or its corollaries of openness, mutual surveillance and mutual interference to the same extent as most European governments now do. The United States's unwillingness to accept the jurisdiction of the International Criminal Court and its relative reluctance about challenge inspections in the CWC are examples of US caution about postmodern concepts. The knowledge that the defence of the civilised world rests ultimately on its shoulders is perhaps justification enough for the US caution.

Besides, as the most powerful country in the world, the USA has no reason to fear any other country and so less reason to accept the idea of security based on mutual vulnerability, except of course in the nuclear field. Here the US is unavoidably vulnerable. Hence one very emphatic piece of postmodern diplomacy in an otherwise rather uncompromising insistence on sovereignty: START[5] and all the other nuclear treaties with Russia – not least the anti-ABM[6] Treaty which is designed to preserve mutual vulnerability. (The occasional bouts of longing for a Strategic Defence Initiative astrodome show, however, that the US is not necessarily reconciled to postmodernism even in the nuclear field.)

Russia poses an important problem for us. Is it going to be a pre-modern, modern or postmodern state? It embodies all three possibilities. A collapse into pre-modernism is perhaps the least likely: the urbanised and industrialised landscape of Russia has a low tolerance for disorder. The risk is more of the state becoming too powerful than of it disappearing altogether. But there are also postmodern elements in Russia trying to get out. And Russian acceptance of the CFE Treaty and of OSCE observers in Chechnya during the first Chechen war, but not during the second, suggests that it is not wholly lost to the doctrine of openness. How Russia behaves in respect of its postmodern treaty commitments will be a critical factor for the future: so will the behaviour of the rest of Europe as it decides how to build its security relationship with Russia.

Of non-European countries, Japan is by inclination a postmodern state. It is not now interested in acquiring territory, nor in using force. It would probably be willing to accept intrusive verification. It is an enthusiastic multilateralist. Were it on the other side of the world, it would be a natural member of organisations such as the OSCE or the EU. Unfortunately for Japan it is a postmodern country surrounded by states firmly locked into an earlier age: postmodernism in one country is possible only up to a point. If China develops in an unpromising fashion (either modern or pre-modern), Japan could be forced to revert to defensive modernism.

And elsewhere? What in Europe has become a reality is in many other parts of the world an aspiration. ASEAN,[7] NAFTA,[8] MERCOSUR,[9] even the OAU[10] suggest at least the desire for a postmodern environment. This wish is unlikely to be realised quickly. Most developing countries are too unsure of their own identity to allow much interference in domestic affairs. Nevertheless, imitation is easier than invention and perhaps rapid postmodernisation could follow the rapid industrialisation that is already under way in many parts of the world. Europe's military power may have declined but the power of example remains. Perhaps that is the postmodern equivalent of imperialism.

THE HEGEMONY OF THE POSTMODERN?

The postmodern group is a powerful and growing collection of states. If we add to that the partially postmodern US and the would-be postmodern Japan it is more or less a dominant group, in economic terms at least. It exerts a strong influence on the way the world is organised. Even those who insist on sovereignty find themselves enmeshed in a range of cooperative institutions and agreements governing trade, transport, communications and so on. Sometimes – as the price of access to financial markets rises – they may find themselves having to accept interference in their economic affairs from the IMF. Those who want trade agreements with the EU find that there is a human rights clause attached.

The strongest of the modern states resist this. China has accepted relatively few binding international commitments; India is notoriously resistant to arrangements that might infringe her sovereignty but most go along with, and all profit from, the multilateral organisation of the world.

The multilateral system that has grown up in the post-war world could be seen as the hegemony of the postmodern. In fact it hardly runs so deep. The multilateral systems concerned are vital to prosperity but, unlike the key treaties in Europe, they are not essential to security. For most non-European states the cooperative world system, though highly beneficial to them in many ways, is resented because it interferes with their full exercise of sovereignty. In a security crisis where state sovereignty was under real threat the multilateral links would place little constraint on violent action; at worse they would simply be blown away.

Thus the image of domestic order and international anarchy is false on one level. The world is in fact a highly structured and orderly system (though without a central authority). On the other hand, anarchy remains the underlying reality in the security field for most parts of the world just as it did in Europe before the First World War despite the high levels of economic interdependence.

In contrast, the cooperative structures in Europe reinforce sovereignty by reinforcing security. Indeed European states now effectively define sovereignty in a different way from hitherto: the state monopoly on lawmaking no longer exists as far as EU members are concerned; and even for others it is limited by as many treaties such as those in the Council of Europe framework. The state monopoly on force is also constrained by alliances, the CFE and other arms controls treaties. In some cases, the monopoly on force has been modified by EU agreements about policing (police are the domestic arm of the monopoly of legitimate force). What in these circumstances does sovereignty amount to for the postmodern state? The answer is probably a mixture of elements: the ability to make and enforce laws is a part of the picture but there is also a second part, which is the right to sit at the table when international cooperative agreements are worked out.

THE POSTMODERN STATE

Lying behind the postmodern international order is the postmodern state – more pluralist, more complex, less centralised than the bureaucratic modern state but not at all chaotic, unlike the pre-modern. As the state itself becomes less dominating, state interest becomes a less determining factor in foreign policy: the media, popular emotion, the interests of particular groups or regions, including transnational groups, all come into play. The deconstruction of the modern state is not yet complete, but it proceeds rapidly: in their different ways the European Community, the movement in many countries towards greater regional autonomy and the more or less universal movement towards privatisation are all part of the process.

Is it fanciful to identify (loosely) the three stages of state development with three types of economy: agricultural in the pre-modern, industrial mass production in the modern, and the post-industrial service and information economy with the postmodern state?

The postmodern state is one that sets value above all on the individual. Hence its unwarlike character. War is essentially a collective activity: the struggles of the twentieth century have been the struggles of liberalism – the doctrine of the individual – against different forms of collectivism: class, nation, race, community, state. In their different ways both fascism and communism were systems designed for war. Fascism was open about it: its ethos and rhetoric – the uniforms, parades, the glorification of war: the state did not just have a monopoly on violence; violence was its *raison d'être*.

Communism also seems, in retrospect, like an attempt to run a state as though it were an army, and as if the country were continuously at war. Not for nothing was the term 'command economy' used.

Both communism and fascism were attempts to resist the break-up of society brought about by the ideas of the enlightenment and the technology of the industrial revolution. Both ideologies tried to provide a refuge for the individual against the loneliness and uncertainty of life in a modernising society. Both tried to use the state to replace the sense of community that was lost as industrial cities replaced agricultural villages (and both thereby maintained *inter alia* the intrusiveness and conformity of the village too: 'Upper Volta with rockets' – was exactly what they aimed at in a way: village life plus state power; technical modernisation in a politically primitive setting). These were thus the culminating points of the modern state – *raison d'état* made into a system of domestic governance as well as foreign policy.

The postmodern state is the opposite. The individual has won[11] and foreign policy becomes the continuation of domestic concerns beyond national boundaries and not vice versa. Individual consumption replaces collective glory as the dominant theme of national life. War is to be avoided; empire is of no interest.

A postmodern order requires postmodern states, and vice versa. To create a lasting postmodern security system in Europe it is crucial that all the most powerful actors should fit into the postmodern pattern. The Cold War could come to an end only through a domestic transformation in the Soviet Union. This is as yet neither complete nor certain, but in historical terms progress has been rapid. What has happened, though, probably irreversibly, is a foreign policy transformation.

Russia has largely given up its empire, joining the rest of Europe as a post-imperial state. The last details of this transition remain to be settled – and this could take a long time. Nevertheless, there is at least a chance that Russia will eventually abandon both imperialist gains and imperialist ambitions. This is important for West European countries. No country can feel safe while their neighbour is under enemy occupation or a regime imposed from the outside. In this sense, security is indivisible.

So long as the Soviet Union tried to maintain territorial control over Poland, and other Central European countries, the possibility of its ambitions stretching further to the West could not be ruled out. Nor need such ambitions be part of a quest for glory or for power; the logic of territorial-based defence is that you always need more territory to defend that which you have acquired ('I have no way to defend my borders except to extend them', said Catherine the Great). As the Soviet Union lost an empire, the West lost an enemy.

For Western Europe, the real postmodern age began in 1989. Until then it was all very well for West European states to operate in the post-modern mode within their own circle, but the dominating theme of their foreign and defence policies for the post-war period was the Cold War. That compelled all of us to base our thinking ultimately on armed protection, secrecy and balance. The hard core of Western policy during this time was ultimately that of the modern state. That is now gone. We are postmodern states living on a postmodern continent. What, then, should we do?

THE IMPLICATIONS FOR SECURITY

The first step is to stop and think. We should recognise that this is a new world but there is neither a new world order – to use the phrase that was fashionable in the early 1990s; nor is there a new world disorder – to use the phrase that has become more fashionable since. Instead there is a zone of safety in Europe, and outside it a zone of danger, and then a zone of chaos.

A world divided into three needs a threefold security policy and a threefold mindset. Neither is easy to achieve.

Before we can think about the security requirements for today and tomorrow, we have to forget the security rules of yesterday. The twentieth century has been marked by absolutes. The war against Hitler and the struggle against communism had to be won. The only possible policy was absolute victory, unconditional surrender.

In the more complex and more ambiguous post-war world, we shall not face the same total threats or need to use the same total war against them. We have to forget, therefore, that the only purpose of the military is to win total victories. In none of the three worlds that we live in will this be appropriate.

SECURITY AND THE POSTMODERN ZONE
There may be no new world order but there is a new European security order. Our task must be to preserve and extend it. Broadly speaking that is what European countries are doing. The task is to promote open democratic institutions, open market economies and open multilateral or transnational diplomacy with as many of our neighbours as possible.

Among ourselves we have to maintain these habits and to improve them with the aim that the key transnational institutions – the EU and NATO – will eventually acquire some of the permanence and solidity that our national institutions enjoy. That means essentially acquiring more loyalty and more legitimacy.

The key question for European security, in the narrow sense, will be how Russia turns out. It must be our central interest to draw Russia into the postmodern European system. That means not just exporting democracy and markets but also bringing Russia into our system of multilateral diplomacy. This cannot be achieved overnight; for the moment, our goal should not be to close off any options. If the Russians decide to retreat to the old system of security by military power, that, regrettably, is their business. Our policy should be to do everything possible to make the alternative course of security by confidence and cooperation – that is to say postmodern security – possible and attractive to them.

Advice for the postmodern state: never forget that more security can be achieved by cooperation than by competition.

SECURITY AND THE MODERN WORLD

Dealing with the modern world, the world of ambitious states, requires a different approach. If eventually these states decide to join a postmodern system of open diplomacy, so much the better; but this will take time, and between now and then lie many dangers. The Gulf War provides an illustration both of the dangers and of how they should be dealt with. One ambitious state attacks another, threatening vital Western interests. In the case of the Gulf War, the interests in question were twofold: first, the maintenance of a plurality of states in an area of the world containing vital oil supplies (in global energy terms this is a policy similar to the traditional British requirement that there should be a plurality of powers on the European continent). The second interest was to ensure that a dangerous and ambitious state did not get its hands on weapons that could ultimately threaten the West itself. Had Saddam Hussein been allowed to retain Kuwait, he would have become the geopolitical master of the Gulf; and the wealth available to him would have financed whatever weapons programme he desired.

The Western response was precisely as it should be: build the most powerful coalition possible, reverse the aggression, punish the aggressor, deal with the weapons programmes. These limited goals required limited means. They did not imply that Iraq should be invaded or occupied or that Saddam Hussein should be removed from power (attractive as that idea undoubtedly was). The reference point for a war of this nature is the eighteenth or nineteenth century, not the twentieth century wars of absolutes. The Gulf War was a war of interests, not a clash of ideologies.

Note that the reasons for fighting this war were not that Iraq had violated the norms of international behaviour. Unfortunately, the reality of the world is that if you invade a country which lies some way outside the vital interests of the powerful, you will probably get away with it. Very likely you will be condemned and your gains will not be recognised (if you choose to keep them); you will lose trust and reputation; you may suffer economic sanctions for a while. But you will not be attacked by the powerful. If India were to invade Nepal, for example, or Argentina Paraguay, it is unlikely that a Gulf War coalition would be put together to reverse the result.

The initial enthusiasm for the idea of a new world order[12] that followed the Gulf War was based on the hope that the United Nations was going to function as originally intended: a world authority policing international law, that is to say a collective-security organisation. In one sense that hope was not unreasonable. The end of the Cold War took us back to 1945. While institutions that had grown up because of, or against the background of, the Cold War, such as NATO or the EU, began to look in need of radical change, the UN was a pre-Cold War institution and, therefore, might become a workable post-Cold War institution. Up to a point this proved to be the case. The UN is more active today than it ever was during the Cold War (between 1946 and 1990 there were 683 Security Council Resolutions; in the period since then there have been more than 350; and, at the same time, there are some 500,000 UN troops in the field today).

The UN is, however, active in peace-keeping and humanitarian work rather than as a collective-security organisation. And a new world order, that at one time attracted hope, was that of a collective-security order.

A collective-security order is one in which the international community enforces international law on recalcitrant states. This would certainly be a new order in the sense that we have never seen anything of the kind in the history of international relations. Unfortunately, we are never likely to see it either.

Some mistook the Gulf War for a war of principles or a collective-security action – and indeed the political rhetoric at the time fostered this impression. In fact, it was a collective defence of interests by the West. The Gulf War was fought to protect an old order, not to create a new one.

In a different sense, though, a collective-security order would not really be new. Collective-security is a combination of two old ideas: stability through balance and stability through hegemony. The *status quo* is maintained by a world body of overwhelming power (the hegemonic element), which throws its weight on the side of a state which is the victim of aggression – the balance-of-power, that is, with the world community as the balancing actor.

This is the old world of state sovereignty in which others do not interfere, of coalitions, of security through military force. The UN, as a collective-security organisation, is there to defend the *status quo* and not to create a new order. And, indeed, the new European order which I have described above is based on entirely different ideas.

The story of the wars in the former Yugoslavia and of the Western intervention there is a more complicated one. The former Yugoslavia contains elements of the post-imperial /pre-modern world where weak states hardly have control over the means of force. There may also be some postmodern aspirations in some of the smaller states. But the dominant feature has been the creation of the modern nation states of Croatia and Serbia.

Western intervention has been above all in support of the individual – humanitarian intervention out of good postmodern motives. But in the end it has run into the ambitions of Milosevic's thoroughly modern nationalistic state. The first major clash, over Bosnia, was eventually handled more or less according to the recipe outlined above for the Gulf War – a mixture of limited force and negotiation – with a certain measure of success. The second episode, in Kosovo, is rather different. Here the humanitarian mission concerned the situation within Serbia. The military campaign was fought – as it turned out entirely with air power – to enforce certain minimum values on a state unwilling to respect them. Unlike the Gulf War this was an action fought for principle and unlike the general rule in postmodern Europe it involved intervention in the domestic affairs of the state not by mutual consent but by force. The basis of this action has been described by the British prime minister in what might be taken as a classic statement of postmodern aspirations:

'We have to enter the new millennium making it known to dictatorships that ethnic cleansing will not be approved. And if we fight it is not for territorial imperatives but for values. For a new internationalism where the brutal repression of ethnic groups will not be tolerated. For a world where those responsible for crimes will have nowhere to hide.'

It is worth quoting at length the most forceful criticism of this approach. Kissinger writes

'The abrupt abandonment of the concept of national sovereignty ... marked the advent of a new style of foreign policy driven by domestic politics and the invocation of universal moralistic slogans.... Those who sneer at history obviously do not recall that the legal doctrine of national sovereignty and the principle of non-interference – enshrined in the UN Charter – emerged at the end of the devastating Thirty Years' War.

'The new discipline of international law sought to inhibit repetition of the depredations of the religious wars of the seventeenth century during which perhaps 40 per cent of the population of Central Europe perished in the name of competing versions of universal truth. Once the doctrine of universal intervention spreads and competing truths contest we risk entering a world in which, in GK Chesterton's phrase, "virtue runs amok"'.[13]

In answer to this, supporters of postmodern intervention would probably argue that they were not, for the moment at least, contemplating universal intervention. But there is a second, more important point: within Europe, perhaps for the first time in 300 years, we do not live in a zone of competing truths. The end of the Cold War has brought with it something like a common set of values in Europe. It is this which makes postmodern intervention feasible in the European context. One of the most striking features of the Kosovo invention was its unanimous support across a group of NATO governments representing every point on the political spectrum.

This does not mean that intervention for values will be easy. It is dangerous to become involved in wars of principle; it is difficult to call them off if they go wrong but equally difficult to sustain them if casualties mount. And besides, war is essentially destructive. One can punish those who transgress principles but it is difficult to use force to implement them. Bombs can flatten cities but they cannot create the rule of law or non-discrimination in employment; troops can keep order but they cannot create a sense of community nor a culture of tolerance.

For the postmodern state there is, therefore, a difficulty. We need to get used to the idea of double standards. Among ourselves, we operate on the basis of laws and open cooperative security. But when dealing with more old-fashioned kinds of state outside the postmodern continent of Europe, we need to revert to the rougher methods of an earlier era – force, pre-emptive attack, deception, whatever is necessary for those who still live in the nineteenth century world of every state for itself.

Advice for postmodern states: those who have friendly, law-abiding neighbours should not forget that in other parts of the world the law of the jungle reigns. Among ourselves, we keep the law but when we are operating in the jungle, we also must use the laws of the jungle. In the coming period of peace in Europe, there will be a temptation to neglect our defences, both physical and psychological. This represents one of the great dangers for the postmodern state.

SECURITY AND THE PRE-MODERN WORLD

What of the pre-modern chaos? What should we do with that? On the basis of a rational calculation of interest, the answer should be: as little as possible. Chaos does not represent a threat, at least not the kind that requires a conventional military response. One may need to bar one's door against its by-products – drugs, disease, refugees – but these are not threats to vital interests that call for armed Western intervention. To become involved in a zone of chaos is risky; if the intervention is prolonged it may become unsustainable in public opinion; if the intervention is unsuccessful it may be damaging to the government that ordered it.

Besides, what form should intervention take? The most logical way to deal with chaos is by colonisation, or hegemony. But this is unacceptable to postmodern states: so if the goal is not colonisation, what should it be? Usually the answer will be that the goals will be ambiguous.

The risk of 'mission creep' is therefore considerable. Those who become involved in the pre-modern world run the risk that ultimately they will be there because they are there. All the conventional wisdom and all realistic doctrines of international affairs counsel against involvement in the pre-modern world.

And yet such 'realistic' doctrines, for all their intellectual coherence, are not realistic. The post-Cold War, postmodern environment is one where foreign policy will be driven by domestic politics; and these will be influenced by the media and by moral sentiment. We no longer live in the world of pure national interest. Human rights and humanitarian problems inevitably play an important part in our policy-making.

A new world order may not be a reality but it is an important aspiration, especially for those who live in a new European order. The wish to protect individuals, rather than to resolve the security problems of states, is a part of the postmodern ethos. In a world where many states suffer breakdowns, there is wide scope for humanitarian intervention. Northern Iraq, Somalia, Yugoslavia[14] and Rwanda are only the beginning of a trend. Operations in these areas are a halfway house between the calculation of interest, which tells you not to get involved, and the moral feeling, which tells the public that something must be done. In different ways, all these operations have been directed towards helping civilians – against the military, the government or the chaos. The results are not always impressive and the interventions are in some respects half-hearted. That is because they live in the ambiguous half-world where interest tells you to stay out and conscience tells you to go in – between Hobbes and Kant.

Such interventions may not solve problems, but they may salve the conscience. And they are not necessarily the worse for that.

Thus we must reconcile ourselves to the fact that we are going to get involved in situations where interest and calculation would tell us to stay out. In this case, there are some rules to observe. The first is to moderate the objectives to the means available. The wars of ideology called for total victory; the wars of interests call for victory; in the pre-modern world victory is not a relevant objective.

Victory in the pre-modern world would mean empire. The postmodern power who is there to save the lives of individual civilians wants to stop short of that. In consequence, goals must be even more carefully defined than in wars of interest. They will be goals of relatives and not of absolutes: more lives saved, lower levels of violence among the local populations; and these must be balanced by low casualties for the interveners. At the same time, we must be prepared to accept, indeed we must expect, failure a good deal of the time. And then we must be prepared to cut our losses and leave. The operation in Somalia was not a success for anybody. And yet it was not unreasonable to try (though perhaps the trial might have been better organised). It gave those responsible in Somalia a breathing space, a chance to sort themselves out. That they failed to take that chance was not the fault of the intervention force. (One attraction of the UN, paradoxically, is that it is able to accept failure, unlike states or the NATO alliance.)

It follows also that when intervening in the pre-modern world, Clausewitz's doctrine still applies: war is the pursuit of politics by other means. Military intervention should always be accompanied by political efforts. If these fail, or if the cost of the military operation becomes too great, then there is no alternative but to withdraw.

Advice to postmodern states: accept that intervention in the pre-modern is going to be a fact of life. To make it less dangerous and more sustainable in the long run, there are four requirements: clear, limited objectives; means, also with clear limits attached to them; a political process to parallel the military operation; and a decision, taken in advance, to withdraw if objectives are not achieved in a given time.

CONCLUSION

This essay is intended to say many things, but especially to say this one thing. That there is no new world order is a common conception. But it is less widely understood that there is a new European order: new in that it is historically unprecedented and also new because it is based on new concepts. Indeed, the order has to a larger extent preceded the concepts. One commentator who fails to understand this – though he understands most other things better than the rest of us and describes them with great elegance and clarity – is Henry Kissinger. 'In a world of players of operationally more or less equal strength, there are only two roads to stability. One is hegemony and the other is equilibrium'.[15] This was the choice in the past, but today it no longer works. Balance is too dangerous; hegemony is no longer acceptable in a liberal world that values human rights and self-determination.

Instead, there is a third possibility. In fact, there have been three sets of alternatives: first came the choice between chaos and empire: instability or hegemony. Then it was a choice between empire and nationalism: hegemony or balance. Finally, today we have a choice between nationalism and integration: balance or openness. Chaos is tamed by empire; empires are broken up by nationalism; nationalism gives way, we hope, to internationalism. At the end of the process is the freedom of the individual; first protected by the state and later protected from the state.

The kind of world we have depends on the kind of states that compose it (see table on page 49): for the pre-modern world, success is empire and failure is disorder; in the modern system, success is balance and failure means falling back into war or into empire. For the postmodern state, success means openness and transnational cooperation. Failure we shall come to in a moment. The open state system is the ultimate consequence of the open society.

This categorisation is not intended to be exclusive – the future is full of surprises (and so indeed is the past). Nor is it intended to represent some inevitable Hegelian progression. Progress it certainly represents, but there is nothing inevitable about it. In particular, there is nothing inevitable about the survival of the postmodern state, in what remains a difficult environment.

The postmodern order faces three dangers. First, there is the danger from the pre-modern. The risk here is one of being sucked in for reasons of conscience and then being unwilling either to conquer or to get out. In the end, the process may be debilitating for morale and dangerous for military preparedness.

In that case the *coup de grâce* would be administered from the modern world. States reared on *raison d'état* and power politics make uncomfortable neighbours for the postmodern democratic conscience. Supposing the world develops (as Kissinger suggests it might) into an intercontinental struggle. Would Europe be equipped for that? That is the second danger – the danger from the modern.

The third danger comes from within. A postmodern world in which security interests are not uppermost in people's minds is one where the state becomes less important. Within the shelter of NATO and the EU we may see a weakening of the states, or a fragmentation – if devolution turns to disintegration. A medieval patchwork of states would be difficult to organise and would probably contain many free riders in the security field.

A postmodern economy can have the result that everyone lives only for themselves, and not at all for the community – the decline of birth rates in the West is already evidence of this tendency. There is a risk too that the deconstruction of the state may spill over into the deconstruction of society. In political terms, an excess of transparency and an over-diffusion of power could lead to a state, and to an international order, in which nothing can be done because there is no central focus of power or responsibility. We may all drown in complexity.

It may be that in Western Europe the era of the strong state – 1648 to 1989 – has now passed, and we are moving towards a system of overlapping roles and responsibilities with governments, international institutions and the private sector all involved but none of them entirely in control. Can it be made to work? We must hope so, and we must try.

NOTES

1. *Scaramouche*, 1952, MGM, Dir. George Sidney.
2. For an excellent general description of the pre-modern state see *Troilus and Cressida*, Act I, Scene iii, 115-124.
3. I am not alone in choosing this terminology, see, for example, Christopher Coker: 'postmodernity and the end of the Cold War,' in *Review of International Studies*, July 1992, or Toulmin S, 1990, *Casomopolis: The hidden agenda of modernity*, University of Chicago Press.
4. *Hamlet*, Act 2, scene ii, 235.
5. Strategic Arms Reduction Treaty.
6. Anti-ballistic missiles.
7. Association of South East Asian Nations.
8. North American Free Trade Area.
9. Mercado Commun del Sud (South America).
10. Organisation of African Unity.
11. Perri 6 of Demos commented on this paragraph: 'the rise of individualism is coincident historically with the rise of organisations. Cultures of individualism are arguably sustainable only in a highly organised society: individualism is not self-sustaining or victorious over other principles of social order'. I agree: this is a useful corrective to balance my possible overstatement. The complex organisational structures that are necessary to sustain individualism coincide exactly with my own picture of the postmodern state.
12. The phrase was in fact used by President Bush in the context of the Gulf War.
13. Kissinger H, 1999, 'Has NATO's success heralrded its own demise?', 16 August 1999.
14. The former Yugoslavia contains elements of pre-modern, modern and even postmodern. It used to be pre-modern (hegemony option), this has dissolved and it is trying to escape from chaos into the modern national state. In Bosnia there are many with postmodern longings.
15. At the 'Britain in the world' conference, 29 March 1995.

	State	Economy	Intellectual basis (Zeitgeist)	Foreign relations
Pre-modern	Where the state functions it will be authoritarian and weak. Control may often break down. State activities most military. Feudal systems and military empires.	Agrarian	Religion, magic scholasticism, religious art and music.	Chaotic, imperial or linked to a religious order. Main objective is acquisition of territory.
Modern — Early	More organised and centralised. Military and diplomatic functions remain central to state but some functions now relate to commerce.	Agrarian/commercial	Rationalist. Hume, Voltaire, Kant, Machiavelli, Pope, Racine, Newton, Leibnitz, Bach, Mozart.	Inter-state relations dominate. Separation of domestic and foreign policy. Commerce becomes a casus belli.
Modern — Late	Centralised and bureaucratic; may be ideological and authoritarian or democratic. Takes responsibility for education, health, welfare, industry, as well as military functions.	Commercial/industrial; mass production	Darwinism, ideas of progress (Hegel, Marx, Treitschke), Clauswitz, Tolstoy, Thomas Mann, Zola, Kipling, Brahms, Mahler.	Nationalistic, era of mass armies and total war.
Modern — Postmodern	Power diffused both domestically and internationally; democratic; much influenced by media and popular emotion. Industrial functions may be reduced. Competing pressures complicate decision making.	Industrial/post-industrial. Services and information industries begin to dominate.	Diversity and uncertainty. Existentialism. Wittgenstein, Camus, Joyce, Einstein, Heisenberg, Warhol.	Transparency and mutual vulnerability; non-state actors including media play an important role. Policy time-frame shortens.